Steve Potter
AND THE ENDERMEN'S STONE

BOOK 1

By Herobrine Books

Copyright © 2015 Herobrine Publishing

All rights reserved. No part of this publication may be reproduced, distributed, or transmitted in any form or by any means, electronic or mechanical, including photocopying, recording, scanning, or by any information storage or retrieval system, without the prior written permission of the publisher, except in the case of brief quotations embodied in critical reviews and certain other non-commercial uses permitted by copyright law.

This unofficial Minecraft novel is an original work of fan fiction which is not sanctioned nor approved by the makers of Minecraft. Minecraft is a registered trademark of, and owned by, Mojang AB, and its respective owners, which do not sponsor, authorize, or endorse this book. All characters, names, places, and other aspects of the game described herein are trademarked and owned by their respective owners.

Chapter 1

Hi. My name is Steve. Steve Potter.

I'm almost eleven years old.

And I am a wizard.

I'm not really a wizard. But I wish I was.

Sometimes I imagine that I have magic powers. Sometimes I even imagine that I have the power to make my toys come to life, or that I can move things with my mind.

But the power I really wish for is the power to fly. Then I would fly as far away from here as I could.

Steve Potter and the Endermen's Stone

You see, right now I live with my aunt and uncle, The Doofuses. And they are really mean.

My uncle Vermin Doofus told me that my parents didn't want me so they left me on here on the doorstep. He always tells me that he didn't want me either, but no one else would take me. So he said he was stuck having to take care of a burden like me.

My Aunt Begonia doesn't like me either. She always reminds me that they could throw me out at any time if I don't behave. She even made Uncle Vermin turn the old broom closet under the stairs into my room instead of giving me a proper room.

But the one that really bothers me is their son, my cousin Dooley Doofus. He's a real bully. Sometimes I wish I had magic powers so I could give him a magical wedgie and pull his underwear over his head.

Steve Potter and the Endermen's Stone

Though, I think my wish for magic powers actually came true one day.

You see, we went to the Zoo to celebrate Dooley's tenth birthday. Uncle Vermin had me carry all of the presents and pick up after all of the other kids at the party.

By the middle of the party I was really tired. But Aunt Begonia said that if I didn't keep on working, she would throw me out on the street.

Later, Dooley and all the kids were looking at a giant spider in a glass tank. And as I was watching, I just imagined the glass disappearing and the spider attacking and eating Dooley whole.

That would be so sweet, I thought.

Steve Potter and the Endermen's Stone

Then, all of a sudden, the glass disappeared!

The giant spider jumped out and landed on Dooley. All of the kids screamed and start running away. Dooley was so scared, he peed his pants.

The Zookeepers came over and took the spider off of Dooley and put it in another cage. When they checked on him, he wasn't moving. I was sure he was dead.

But, he had just fainted.

Steve Potter and the Endermen's Stone

I was just standing there, with a big smile on my face, when Uncle Vermin came over and said, "You had something to do with this, didn't you, Steve?!! Just wait till we get home!"

Normally I would be really scared. But this was the best day ever.

Chapter 2

The good thing was that my birthday was coming up soon. I was going to turn eleven years old.

But I didn't think Uncle Vermin or Aunt Begonia were going to have a party for me. Knowing them, they were probably going to hand me a candle and tell me how grateful I should be that I got that much.

But, a few days later, a letter arrived for me.

I couldn't believe it. I had never received a letter before.

Steve Potter and the Endermen's Stone

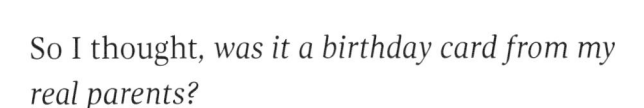

So I thought, *was it a birthday card from my real parents?*

As soon as I was about to open it, Uncle Vermin took it, ripped it up and threw it in the garbage.

It made me really sad. Then it made me really mad.

Then, all of a sudden, we heard a weird sound. It started getting louder and louder. It sounded like a giant wave was about to hit our house.

Next thing I know, a bunch of letters rushed into the house through the fireplace and every door and window. It filled the whole house with hundreds of letters flying all over the place.

Uncle Vermin and Aunt Begonia ran for cover.

I started laughing.

Steve Potter and the Endermen's Stone

I think I am a wizard, I thought.

As soon as I grabbed one of the letters and was about to open it, Uncle Vermin grabbed it and ripped it up. Then he sent me to my room.

Uncle Vermin and Aunt Begonia collected all of the letters and burned them.

I really wish someone would come and rescue me from this crazy family, I thought.

Chapter 3

The day before my birthday, Uncle Vermin and Aunt Begonia took me to a shack on a faraway island somewhere.

When we got there, they started acting really weird. The way they peeked through the window every few minutes, I thought we were hiding from someone.

Suddenly, we heard banging on the door. Uncle Vermin and Aunt Begonia got really scared.

"No one's home. Go away," Uncle Vermin said.

Steve Potter and the Endermen's Stone

All of a sudden the door blew open and it knocked Uncle Vermin to the floor. Then I saw a giant figure standing at the door.

The giant figure walked inside and stomped really loudly with his feet. When I looked at him in the light, he was about seven feet tall, and covered in a big cloak. When he took off the hood, his head was almost totally covered with hair.

Steve Potter and the Endermen's Stone

He lifted up his hand, and I thought he was going to crush me with one blow.

"Happy Birthday, Steve!" he said.

"What?" I said in surprise.

"Happy Birthday!" he said again. "It is your birthday, isn't it?"

"No, that's tomorrow," I said.

"Well, better early than never. Here you go."

He handed me a cupcake with a small lighted candle on it.

"Just make a wish and blow out the candle," he said.

I wish that I could be taken far away from here to go on a wonderful and magic adventure, I thought.

Then I blew out the candle.

Chapter 4

"What's your name?" I asked the giant.

"My name is Rabius Haggish. I came to pick you up to bring you to school."

"What school?" I asked him.

"You've been accepted to Hogcrafts School of Magic and Witchcraft," he said. "Didn't you get your admission letter?"

I shook my head no.

Haggish gave Uncle Vermin and Aunt Begonia a really mean look.

"Well, here you go," he said as he pulled out a letter from one of his pockets.

Steve Potter and the Endermen's Stone

I read the letter out loud and it said:

Congratulations Steve Potter!

You've been accepted to Hogcrafts School of Magic and Witchcraft.

Prepare yourself for a wonderful adventure full of magic and miracles in the land of Minecraft.

We have been waiting for you a long time, Steve.

And we are very excited for your visit.

Signed,
Argus Bumbledorf

HOGCRAFTS
School of Magic and Witchcraft

I couldn't believe it. My wish had come true!

Steve Potter and the Endermen's Stone

I was finally going to be the wizard that I always wanted to be.

Not to mention, I was going to a really cool place full of adventure and magic.

What was the name of it again? Oh, yeah...

The land of Minecraft.

Chapter 5

Haggish told me that I had to get prepared for wizard school, so he decided to take me to the city to get some school supplies.

"I'm sure your parents would've been really proud of you, now that you're going to Hogcrafts School of Magic and Witchcraft. I really miss them sometimes," he said as he wiped a tear from his eye.

"You knew my parents?" I asked Haggish. "But, Uncle Vermin and Aunt Begonia said that my parents didn't want me so they abandoned on their doorstep."

"Oh, Steve. Your parents loved you very much. And they didn't leave you. Unfortunately, your parents were killed by an evil wizard named Lord Baldywarts," Haggish said.

All of a sudden, I heard a loud clap of thunder.

Wow. I knew my parents loved me! Uncle Vermin and Aunt Begonia were just lying to me.

But I was really sad to hear they were killed.

"Who is Lord *Baldywarts*?" I asked Haggish.

Then, I heard another clap of thunder.

Wait a minute. Let me try that again...

"Baldywarts."

CLAPBOOM!

"Baldywarts."

CLAPBOOM!

"Ba, ba, ba, de, de, wart, wart, wart..."

CLAP, CLAP, CLAP, BOOM, BOOM, CL-CL-CL-CLAP!

Man, this is fun! I thought.

"Steve, don't do that. You don't want anyone to find out you're a wizard, do you?" Haggish asked.

"Oh, Sorry."

"Well, just know that your parents died trying to protect you," Haggish said. "And they succeeded too, because the only thing, *you know who*, could do to you, was give you that scar on your forehead."

My scar! I always wondered why I had this on my head.

Though, I always tried to cover it up because it looked funny. I thought it looked like an

Steve Potter and the Endermen's Stone

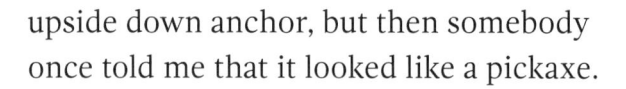

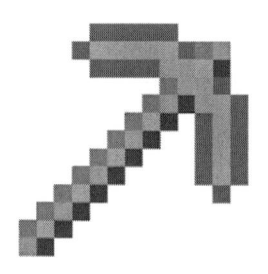

upside down anchor, but then somebody once told me that it looked like a pickaxe.

Now I finally know where it came from.

"So where is, *you know who* now, Haggish?" I asked him.

"Some say he died. Others say that he is just a spirit, roaming around the earth trying to find a way to be made whole again," he said.

"Do you think he's going to come after me again?" I asked Haggish.

Steve Potter and the Endermen's Stone

"Well, that's why we are going to train you to be a wizard, Steve. And you are going to be the best wizard that has ever lived," Haggish said.

Wow, I'm going to be a wizard. This is so awesome.

Chapter 6

As we were walking through the city, I wondered where a kid would go to get school supplies to prepare for a school of Magic and Witchcraft.

"So where are we going to get my school supplies, Haggish?" I asked him.

"We're going to a very special place in the city," Haggish said with a twinkle in his eye. "It's a place that only Hogcrafts wizards and witches in training go," he said.

"Really? What's it called?" I asked.

"We're going to a special place called GameStop."

Steve Potter and the Endermen's Stone

GameStop! Wow I always knew that place was magical. When Uncle Vermin and Aunt Begonia would take me and Dooley shopping for clothes (well mostly Dooley), every time I passed GameStop I could tell there was something special about that place.

When we got to GameStop, Haggish and I entered the store.

Haggish gave the store clerk a subtle nod, and the store clerk gave Haggish a nod back.

Then the store clerk closed the front door and put the CLOSED sign in the window. The store clerk then pulled out a golden key and opened a panel behind his counter, which revealed a big glowing button. He pushed the button and I heard a rumbling sound.

All of sudden, the entire wall of video game cases on the right slid back and away, and another wall with a giant screen and console slid into its place.

Steve Potter and the Endermen's Stone

On the screen, a big banner popped up that said, "MINECRAFT."

While I watched, Haggish started playing the game and brought up this big list of Inventory Items.

"Well, let me see what you're going to need this semester," he said as he looked at his long list.

"Hmmm, you'll need a crafting table, pickaxe, shovel, some coal, some iron... A book and quill... Can't forget the enchanting table… A few torches… And last but not least, you'll need a wand!"

"A wand? What will I need that for?" I asked Haggish.

"Steve, a wand is a wizard's most powerful weapon… You must never leave home without it!" he said.

Whoa.

Then he exited the game.

"Well, there you go, Steve. You have everything you need for your first semester. I'll come back in a few weeks to pick you up and take you to school," he said.

So he brought me back home and said goodbye.

Wow, I can't believe I'm going to train to be a wizard.

This has got to be the best birthday ever!

Chapter 7

A month later, Haggish came and picked me up to take me to the train station.

When we got to the train station, Haggish handed me a ticket.

"Here you go, Steve. This is your ticket to get on the train," he said.

I looked at the ticket and noticed something strange.

"Haggish, this ticket says that I need to go to Minecraft Platform Release 1.8," I said. "What does that mean?"

MINECRAFT
Platform 1.8

"Whoa. You got the latest Release edition. That's really good, Steve. Usually you'll get a ticket for one of the early releases like 1.7 or even 1.0," Haggish said. "1.0, now that was a real clunker."

I really didn't know what Haggish was talking about, so I just played along.

Haggish walked me to the gate and then he said his goodbyes. He said he had some important business to attend to for Professor Bumbledorf.

Professor Bumbledorf, I thought, *I remember that name. That was the name that was on my acceptance letter.*

Steve Potter and the Endermen's Stone

So, after leaving Haggish, I walked for a while until I got to Platform 1.

I looked around and saw Platform 2, but I couldn't find Platform 1.8.

I decided to ask the conductor of the train.

"Excuse me, Mr. Conductor sir, I see Platform 1, and Platform 2 is over there, but I don't see Platform 1.8," I said.

"Are you trying to be funny? Go on, get out of here, kid. This is not a place for playing games!" he said in a stern voice.

So I walked away from him as confused as ever.

Then I heard a family walk past me and mention that they were going to Platform 1.8.

Steve Potter and the Endermen's Stone

"Mom, I'm so excited," the kid said. "I can't wait to see Hogcrafts School of Magic and Witchcraft!"

"I'm happy for you too, Run. Just hurry up and get to Platform 1.8 before the train leaves."

"Oh, OK, Mom. Here I go!"

Next thing I know an express train came speeding through the tracks, and this kid backed up, got a running start, and then ran straight into the moving train! He totally disappeared.

Whoa! That was awesome. But if I try that I'm going to kill myself. I better ask his Mom how to do it.

"Excuse me, Ma'am. Do you know how to get to Platform 1.8?" I asked her.

"This is your first time in Minecraft is it? Well, you are in for an exciting time," she said. "Now what you need to do is push off really fast, and as soon as the express train rushes through the station, you jump right on."

I heard the next express train about to rush through the station. So I positioned myself and my cart full of luggage, and I pushed off really fast.

As I was running, the only thought I had was, *this is going to be awesome... If I don't die, that is.*

As soon as I got closer to the rushing train, my heart started beating faster and faster.

Then right before I got to the speeding train, I closed my eyes.

Next thing you know, I went right through the train's outside wall! It was amazing!

But what was even more amazing was what I saw on the other side...

Chapter 8

All of a sudden, I was on the train.

But this was no ordinary train. It wasn't even an ordinary world!

Everything looked so different. It looked as if everything was made of blocks, kind of like Lego blocks. I saw people in the train with square heads and long rectangular bodies. I looked out the window of the train and the clouds were rectangular, and the sun was a perfect square!

I started feeling dizzy, so I went into an empty train cabin and sat down.

Could I be inside of a video game? I thought.

Then I was startled by the square headed conductor that walked in through the door.

"Ticket please!" he said.

"Oh, yeah," I said as I fumbled for my ticket. I handed it to him and he punched it.

He noticed the dazed look on my face and said, "First time in Minecraft, eh? Don't worry, you'll get used it. And the dizziness will wear off real soon. Here, this will help."

He handed me what looked like a golden apple. I didn't eat breakfast, so I accepted the apple and took a big bite out of it.

All of a sudden, I felt much better.

Steve Potter and the Endermen's Stone

"Much better, eh?" the conductor asked. "But if you think this is weird, wait till you get to Hogcrafts School of Magic and Witchcraft," he said knowingly. "That place will really cook your noodle."

Then he walked away to punch more tickets.

As I was finishing the apple, the boy from the platform walked in. Except now he had a square head and a rectangular body. I could only tell it was the same boy from the platform because he had really red hair.

"Hey, can I sit here with you? All of the other cabins are taken," he said.

"Sure," I said.

"My name is Run, Run Weasel," he said.

I thought, *Run Weasel? That is the funniest name I had ever heard.*

I tried not to laugh, but it was really hard keeping it in.

"He, he, snicker, ha, ha, ha!"

"Yeah, I know, my name is really dumb. I still don't know why my parents named me that," he said. "What's your name?"

"Me?" (snicker) "My name is Steve, Steve Potter."

"Whoa, no way! So it is true. You're the famous Steve Potter! It's really great to meet you. I've heard so much about you," Run said.

"You've heard about me?" I said, thinking he made a mistake.

"Yeah, you're the kid that got attacked by, you know who, and lived. My Mom and Dad always tell me bedtime stories about you."

I thought, *whoa, people tell bedtime stories about me?*

"Ooh, ooh, can I see your scar?" Run asked me.

"Sure," I said and I showed him my scar. Run's eyes got really big when he saw it.

"Looks like a pickaxe," he said.

All of a sudden, a girl came by the door of the cabin. It was hard to tell it was a girl, but the hair on her square head was longer than Run's.

Steve Potter and the Endermen's Stone

"Has anyone seen an ocelot run by here by any chance? One of the other boys lost it, and he's crying his eyes out because he can't find it," she said.

"No," Run and I both said.

"By the way, my name is Herobriney, Herobriney Stranger," she said.

"HE-RO-BRINEE?" said Run. "What kind of name is that?"

Steve Potter and the Endermen's Stone

"It's pronounced 'HERBRINEE' thank you, and I would appreciate you saying it like that," she said with a bit of an attitude.

"My name is Steve Potter."

"Wow, so it is true. You're going to be in our class at Hogcrafts School of Magic and Witchcraft," she said. "Well, Steve, it will be a pleasure being classmates with you. I wish I could stay and chat, but right now I have to go find an ocelot. Good bye, Steve. Goodbye..." she said as she looked at Run.

"Name is Run, Run Weasel."

(Snicker, snicker), "Good bye, Run Weasel," she said as she walked away.

A few seconds later, we heard her burst out laughing down the corridor.

Chapter 9

When we arrived at our train stop, it was already evening.

It was my first night in Minecraft and it was really weird. The moon was square, and the rectangular clouds gave it a really eerie look.

But I didn't mind because I was just so excited to see what Hogcrafts School of Magic and Witchcraft looked like.

The teachers walked us down a long path through the woods to get to the lake where boats would be waiting for us.

Steve Potter and the Endermen's Stone

"Make sure you stay on the path," one of the teachers said. "There are dangerous creatures out at night, and you best not be caught out in the woods by yourself."

Right after he said that, we heard a weird noise in the woods.

"UUURRRGGHH!"

All the kids were scared. And I have to admit, so was I.

When we got to the lake, we took the boats over to the island and school.

As I was riding in the boat with the other kids, I could see the school in the distance. It looked like a giant castle made out of Lego blocks. It really looked amazing. I had only seen a castle in the movies, but this was real and it was huge.

Steve Potter and the Endermen's Stone

When we got there, we all went up a giant staircase and found another teacher was waiting for us.

"Welcome students," she said. "We are very proud to have you attend the most prestigious Magic and Witchcraft School in the entire Overworld."

"She's a witch," Run whispered in my ear.

"How do you know?" I asked him.

"Well, my brothers, who were students here before me, said that if she has a funny hat with a buckle and a big nose with a mole on it, then she is definitely a witch," Run said. "They even said that they think all of her magic comes from that mole."

"My name is Professor MeGottago," the witch said.

All of a sudden the kids were snickering and laughing under their breath. One of the kids even burst out laughing.

"What is your name, young man?" the witch lady said sternly.

"My name is Norbert, Norbert Longerbottom," he said. Then the kids started snickering and laughing when they heard him say his name.

"Well, Mr. Longerbottom," she said. "You shouldn't make fun of your teachers."

Then she waved her wand, and all of a sudden, Norbert's bottom started growing longer and longer. It kept on growing until it touched the floor.

All the kids burst out laughing. I tried to hold it in but I couldn't, and I burst out laughing too.

"That will teach you to make fun of your teachers," Professor. MeGottago said. "But don't worry; it will wear off in a few hours."

She waved her wand up and our whole group went quiet. I think none of us wanted to have Professor MeGottago turn us into our names.

Steve Potter and the Endermen's Stone

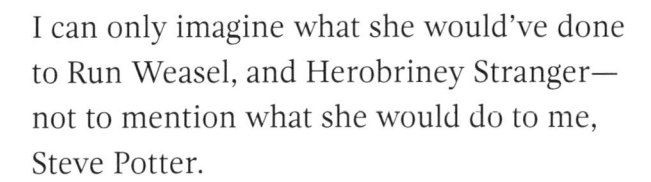

I can only imagine what she would've done to Run Weasel, and Herobriney Stranger—not to mention what she would do to me, Steve Potter.

"Now you will all enter the great hall, and you will be sorted into the house you will be in for the rest of the semester," she said. "You will either be in Griffendork, Hagglepuff, Ravenflaw or Spideryn."

Then she opened the doors and we walked into a big banquet room. It looked like a giant lunch room with big long tables made out of wood. The whole room was lit by hundreds of torches that floated in the middle of the air. It was awesome.

Professor MeGottago walked us in a straight line to a really big, square, leather helmet that was lying on a chair in the front of the room.

Professor MeGottago pulled out a long list and started reading out names.

"Herobriney Stranger," she said.

Herobriney walked up to the helmet, and Ms. MeGottago took the helmet and put it on her head. All of a sudden the helmet grew eyes and a big mouth! It was the scariest thing I ever saw.

Steve Potter and the Endermen's Stone

Next thing I know, the helmet yells out, "GRIFFENDORK!"

All the kids started cheering.

"Next is... Run Weasel," Professor MeGottago said, and the kids started snickering when they heard his name. She gave us all a look that quieted the whole group really fast.

Run walked up to the chair, and Ms. MeGottago put the leather helmet monster on his head.

"GRIFFENDORK!" it yelled.

The kids let out a big cheer for Run.

After about five or six kids, she called my name.

"Steve Potter."

I walked up to the chair and Ms. MeGottago put that thing on my head. I could feel it rubbing my scalp like it was licking my head.

It felt weird, but I was just thinking about wanting to be picked to go to Griffendork.

"OH, A SPECIAL ONE, EH? THIS ONE HAS A LOT OF POTENTIAL. SPIDERYN WOULD BE GOOD FOR YOU," it said.

"Please say Griffendork, please say Griffendork," was all I could whisper under my breath.

"GRIFFENDORK!!!"

The kids all cheered for me, and boy did it feel good.

"Next up… Drago Mouthwash!"

Up comes this tall, white haired, mean looking boy that looked like a square headed vampire.

"That's Malfwalsh!" he said as he gave a mean look to all the kids that were even thinking of laughing at him.

Professor MeGottago put the leather helmet thing on his head, and it made a face like it knew an evil secret that we didn't.

"SPIDERYN!!!"

A whole group of other mean looking kids started cheering.

Steve Potter and the Endermen's Stone

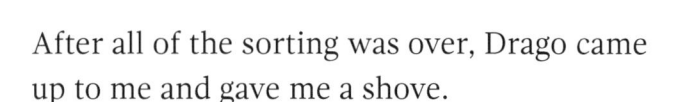

After all of the sorting was over, Drago came up to me and gave me a shove.

"So you're Steve Potter, huh? You're a lot shorter than all the stories say," he sneered. "I guess I'm going to have to show you who the real wizard is around here."

Then he walked away laughing.

Run, Herobriney and I just looked at each other and said, "Yeah, that guy is going to be trouble."

Chapter 10

My first week of class was a lot of fun.

In my Transformation class, Professor MeGottago taught us how to turn animals into water cups. It was really cool. Run had some problems turning his animal into a cup, though. He tried to turn a pig into a water cup but instead ended up with some pieces of cooked ham.

In my Enchanting class, we had to make a chicken feather fly. No one could do it, except for Herobriney. She was the only one who could pronounce the spell right.

"Minecraftium Levitatia!" she said, and her feather started floating up into the air until it touched the ceiling.

Steve Potter and the Endermen's Stone

Norbert Longerbottom had such a hard time doing it, that instead of making the feather fly, he turned it back into a chicken.

...then he blew up the chicken.

The class I was really looking forward to was the Defense of Evil class. It was supposed to be the coolest class in the whole school. I heard they would teach us cool stuff like how to battle evil mobs like Skeletons and Creepers, even spiders.

When I got to class, though, it didn't seem as good as everyone said it was. I think it was because it was taught by a really mousey teacher named Professor Squirrel. He even looked like a Squirrel. He also had the biggest head of mussed up hair that I had ever seen. It looked like a giant bird's nest.

He mostly talked about how to build a shelter at night, and how to run and hide if you are ever attacked by a Skeleton.

"This guy is really dull," Run said. "My brothers told me that in their Defense of Evil class they learned how to do jump attacks, and how to do inflict critical damage, and stuff. The only attack this guy is going to teach us is how to bore mobs to death."

I laughed.

But, the teacher that really scared me was my Hogcrafts Potions Brewing teacher Professor Snoop.

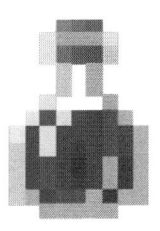

Even walking into his class I could tell that I was going to have a hard time.

Steve Potter and the Endermen's Stone

When our class started, he said, "I see we have a celebrity in our midst. Mr. Potter, it's good for you to join us. Can you please tell us, Mr. Potter, how do you create a Potion of Healing to protect yourself from a cave spider bite?"

"I don't know," I said.

"How do you create a Potion of Fire Resistance to prevent yourself from getting burned while crossing a lava pit?"

"I don't know," I said.

"How would one create a Potion of Water Breathing to save one's self from drowning?"

"I don't know," I said.

"Well, it seems you're not the celebrity everyone thinks you are, are you, Mr. Potter?" he said with a sneer.

Man, being in Brewing class was really embarrassing.

Steve Potter and the Endermen's Stone

For some reason Professor Snoop really had it out for me.

But I had no idea why.

Later that day, I ran into Haggish.

"How's your first week of school going, Steve?" he asked.

"It's been really good," I said. "All my classes are really fun. And my teachers are really great too… All except for Professor Snoop."

"What's wrong with Snoop?" Haggish asked.

"Well, I think Professor Snoop hates me. But I don't know why," I said.

"Professor Snoop hates everybody, Steve," Haggish said. "He's just one of those lonely souls that only finds comfort in the misery of others. Don't let him worry you any."

"I'll try not to," I said. "By the way, what brings you to school today, Haggish?"

"I'm on a secret mission for Professor Bumbledorf. But I can't tell you what it is, so don't ask me," he said.

I could tell Haggish wasn't good at keeping secrets. He reminded me of my cousin Dooley. Whenever I needed to know whether my Uncle Vermin and Aunt Begonia were going to punish me for something, I could always get it out of Dooley.

"It's OK, Haggish," I said. "I already know what it is… Did you get it already, by the way?"

"How did you know about the Endermen's Stone?!! I didn't tell a soul, I swear," he said. "Oh no. Professor Bumbledorf is going to be so mad at me for telling another one of his secrets."

"Don't worry, Haggish," I said. "Your secret is safe with me."

Then Haggish walked me over to my next class.

Chapter 11

I was really excited about my first flying class.

I thought we were going to ride broomsticks or magic carpets or something like that. Boy was I wrong. It seems that one of the teachers got the crazy idea that riding a flying pig was a better idea.

Now, I thought being in Minecraft was weird, but this was really crazy.

So our teacher, Professor Pooch, had us put some magic saddles on these cute little pigs.

Steve Potter and the Endermen's Stone

"Now get on your pigs, and once you are ready, I want you to say 'Up' really loud," she said. "Ready, go!"

We got on our pigs and yelled "Up." But, for some reason it didn't work. We must have yelled, "Up" for about ten minutes, but none of us were able to get our pigs to fly.

Then all of a sudden, Norbert Longerbottom's pig began to float higher and higher. Next thing you know, he got up really high, and then the pig started darting and dashing really fast through the sky.

We thought he was going to die for sure.

Professor Pooch tried to talk him down but he was going too fast. She finally got him to come down for a landing, but he was going so fast, that whatever landing he was going to have was going to hurt.

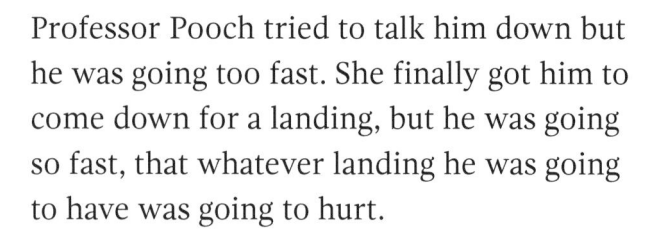

Finally, the pig landed on the ground, but Norbert kept going and plowed right into the grass. When we caught up to him his head was buried in the ground, and his bottom was sticking up.

"I don't think Ms. MeGottago's spell has worn off yet," Drago said. And all the other kids started laughing at Norbert.

When Norbert got up, he had a mouth full of grass.

"Oh dear, let's go take you to the infirmary," Professor Pooch said.

"Ha, ha, ha… That's what he gets for being such a dummy," Drago said.

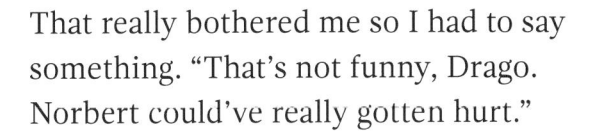

That really bothered me so I had to say something. "That's not funny, Drago. Norbert could've really gotten hurt."

"What's the matter, Potter, afraid of a little danger?" he said. Then Drago gave me a really big shove that sent me to the floor.

I was really mad and about to give him a shove back when Drago jumped on his pig and flew away really fast. I wasn't going to let him get away with that so I jumped on my pig and I went after him.

Drago was zigging and zagging through the sky like he had been flying pigs in Minecraft for a long time. I don't know why, but flying felt really natural to me too. I zigged when he zigged, and I zagged when he zagged. When he went up, I went after him, and when he came down, I dropped down real easy. I felt like I had done this before. It was incredible.

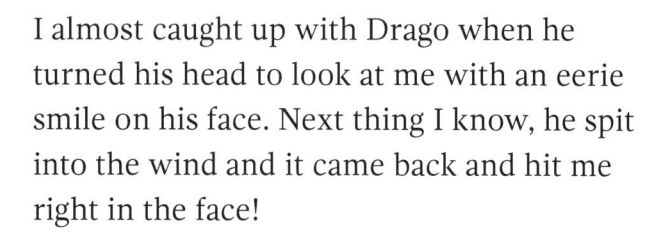

I almost caught up with Drago when he turned his head to look at me with an eerie smile on his face. Next thing I know, he spit into the wind and it came back and hit me right in the face!

Ugh! It was so nasty that I lost control of my pig. I started falling really fast, and was about to do a nose dive into the ground like Norbert.

All of a sudden, Professor MeGottago appeared below me, waved her hand, and stopped me and my pig in the air. Then she brought us both down safely.

I tried to explain to Professor MeGottago that Drago shoved me first, but she raised her hand with the wand, so I shut up really quick. She just told me to follow her.

We walked down the school halls until we got to another classroom. I thought it was the detention room, or maybe a torture chamber or something.

Steve Potter and the Endermen's Stone

She walked into a full classroom and said, "I'm sorry Professor Squirrel, but can I please speak to Markus Wood?"

Then a tall, athletic boy came out of the class.

"Markus, I want to introduce you to Steve Potter. I think we've found our new Creeper for the Quibblitch team. Steve, Markus is our Quibblitch captain," she said.

"Quibblitch, what's that?" I asked.

"Quibblitch is the deadliest game ever known in Minecraft," Markus said with a scary look on his face. "Just kidding. Quibblitch is like soccer but on flying pigs. Lots of fun...if you don't kill yourself."

I was really scared there for a moment.

"Welcome aboard, Steve. We're happy to have you as our new Creeper," Markus said.

Man, I thought, *I wonder what I've gotten myself into.*

Chapter 12

After class, I told Run and Herobriney the good news that I was going to be the new Creeper for Griffendork.

"Bloody smell, Steve! That makes you the youngest student to ever be a Creeper," Run said.

"It's in his blood," Herobriney said, as she pointed to the old trophy case in the halls outside of our classroom.

There in the trophy case was a huge trophy with the name "STEVE POTTER - CREEPER" on it.

"This was my dad's trophy!"

"That's right. It seems you have wizardry in your blood," Herobriney said.

All of a sudden, Drago walked up to us and said to Herobriney, "That's better than I can say for you, you little Muttblood."

Herobriney started to tear up. I got really angry and was about to sock Drago in the nose. But I knew if I did I would get expelled.

"What are you going to do about it, Potter?" he said.

My blood was boiling as I stared him down.

"Come on, you guys, let's get out of here," Run said to me and Herobriney.

As I was walking away, Drago said, "I challenge you to a wizard's duel, tonight at midnight at the great hall."

"I accept!" I said, knowing that I shouldn't have.

"Steve, don't do it. Drago is just trying get you expelled. If they catch you after hours, you're definitely going to get in trouble," Herobriney said.

"Someone needs to put that guy in his place!" Run said.

"Yeah," I said, even though I was totally terrified.

Later, at midnight, Run, Herobriney and I went to the great hall to face Drago for our wizard's duel.

I had never been in a wizard's duel, so I knew I was going to die.

"Remember to wave your wand really high, Steve," Herobriney said. "And don't forget to pronounce your spells really clearly. And don't forget to…"

"Steve's going to be fine. Stop nagging him," Run said.

"It's OK. I need all of the help I can get," I said.

We had to sneak into the great hall so that Mr. Filth, the groundskeeper, didn't see us. His real name is Mr. Firth, but for some reason he's really dirty and smelly all of the time. So the kids just call him Mr. Filth.

We had to avoid Mr. Filth's pet cat too. The other kid's say that Mr. Filth's cat can talk and tells him everything it sees.

When we got to the great hall, no one was there.

"I knew it, Steve," Herobriney said. "It was a trick. Drago was just trying to get you in trouble."

Steve Potter and the Endermen's Stone

All of a sudden we heard a sound outside of the door.

"Who's in there?!!"

"It's Mr. Filth! Let's get out of here!" Run said.

We all ran out of the great hall through a back door. We ran as fast as we could, but we ended up getting lost.

"Where are we?" Run asked.

"I think we're in the West Wing," Herobriney said. "This area is supposed to be forbidden. So if Mr. Filth catches us, were going to be expelled for sure."

Suddenly we heard some footsteps and a loud meow like the sound of a cat.

"There's a door," I said, "let's go in that one."

So we opened the door. It was really heavy, and it looked like it was made out of some kind of rock. Then we closed the door behind us, and pressed our ears to the door to hear if Mr. Filth was coming.

"I think he's gone," Herobriney said.

Next thing you know, we hear Run whimpering next to us.

"What's the matter with you now, Run?" Herobriney asked impatiently.

Herobriney and I turned around and we were terrified by what we saw.

There was a huge three headed monster hovering above us. All of a sudden it started making a popping noise, and then it started shooting monster skull heads at us!

We dodged the exploding monster heads and pulled the door open, scampering through. We slammed it behind us as fast as we could.

We ran as fast as we could until we found the door that led to the Griffendork house.

Steve Potter and the Endermen's Stone

When we finally stopped running, Run said, "What the bloody smell, was that?!!"

"That was a Wither," Herobriney said. "But I don't understand what it's doing in this school. Withers are supposed to be extremely dangerous creatures that have been known to destroy entire villages."

"Maybe it was protecting something," I said. "Did you see the trap door under where it was hovering?"

"Well, whatever it was, it sure scared me!" Run said.

"What's that smell?" Herobriney asked.

"I told you... Whatever that thing was, it sure scared me!" Run said.

Chapter 13

A few weeks later, Run, Herobriney and I were getting ready for the Halloween ball they had at school every year.

Run decided to dress up like Professor Bumbledorf. He taped a bunch of cotton balls to his face, and put on a really big wizard's hat.

Herobriney decided to dress up like Ms. MeGottago. She got a big witch's hat and some high heeled shoes with buckles. I think she was trying to score some brownie points so she could get a good grade in her class.

I decided to dress up like Mr. Filth. It was easy. All I had to do was roll around in the mud outside, and then make a cat out of an old mop.

We entered the great hall to find it was transformed into a Halloween Haunted House.

It was really scary, and amazing at the same time. There were jack-o-lanterns floating in the air with candles in them, and there were skeletons walking around serving food. There were even real ghosts flying around everywhere.

"Hey, Run, I thought you said that Skeletons are evil and want to hurt kids in Minecraft?" I asked.

"Most of them are," Run said. "But my brothers said that if you catch one you can make it into a pet. They said they caught one once, but the legs got away. So they only had half a skeleton. Wasn't really good for much, so my brothers made it into a coat hanger."

"Whoa," I said.

"Hey, where's Herobriney?" I asked Run.

"She said that she had to fix her witch's hat or something. She went to the girl's bathroom."

All of a sudden, Mr. Squirrel ran into the great hall and yelled, "ZOMBIE!!!" Then he fainted.

All of the kids started screaming and yelling, and running around all over the place.

Then somebody yelled, "SILENCE!!!"

It came from Professor Bumbledorf. "Teachers, take all of the students to their houses. The rest of us will look into this Zombie business," he said.

As they rushed us to our houses, I remembered that Herobriney was still in the bathroom.

"Run, we need to get Herobriney. She doesn't know about the Zombie," I said.

"Let's hurry. She went to the bathroom upstairs, because the one downstairs was out of order," Run said.

So we hurried upstairs, but right before we got to the door, we heard a really loud scream.

Steve Potter and the Endermen's Stone

"AAAAAAAHHH!!!!"

All of a sudden we heard a smashing sound. We ran into the bathroom and right in front of us was the biggest, ugliest Zombie you could imagine.

"Run, Steve, help me!" Herobriney pleaded, crouched in a corner.

"UUURRRGGHHHH!!!" the monster said.

Steve Potter and the Endermen's Stone

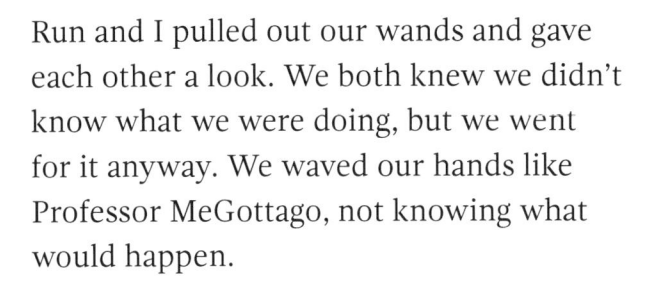

Run and I pulled out our wands and gave each other a look. We both knew we didn't know what we were doing, but we went for it anyway. We waved our hands like Professor MeGottago, not knowing what would happen.

All of a sudden, the Zombie's bottom got longer and longer until it slunk to the floor.

"UURRGHH?!!"

"We must've done the Longerbottom spell," Run said.

Whatever we did, it worked! The Zombie's butt was so heavy that it couldn't move very far. All it could do was swing its long arms at us.

We ran over and got Herobriney, and the three of us ran toward the door. Right when we got there, Professor MeGottago and Professor Snoop burst in. They looked at us and then the zombie, and then us again, surprised. Professor MeGottago waved her wand really high and said, "CADAVEROUS PETRIFICOUS!!!"

Next thing we know, the Zombie turned to stone.

Herobriney sagged in relief as Run and I let out our breaths.

"Man that was close," Run said, shaking his head. "Thank you, Professor MeGottago."

"Don't thank me. All of you are in real trouble. You were supposed to be in your rooms. Why did you try to take on a full grown Mutant Zombie by yourselves?"

"It was my fault, Professor MeGottago," Herobriney said. "I thought I had learned enough to take on the Zombie all by myself. But I was wrong. And if it wasn't for Steve and Run, I would probably be dead."

"Well, I will have to dock you three health points for trying something so foolish," Professor MeGottago said. "And as for the two of you boys, you both lose one health point each for trying to fight a Zombie without a teacher."

Run and I were both really sad.

"But," she said, "you each get two health points for being brave enough to face a full grown Mutant Zombie, and coming to the aid of your fellow student. Now off to bed you go!"

Run and I smiled at each other, but we felt bad for Herobriney.

Then we left to go to our rooms. But before I turned away, I noticed that Professor Snoop had a big burn on his arm. He saw me looking and covered it up just as I saw it.

Then it made me think that Professor Snoop probably had something to do with the Mutant Zombie.

Figures. He probably brought it into the school to come eat me, I thought.

Chapter 14

My first Quibblitch match was really scary.

I had never played any sports in my life, and now I was supposed to be one of the most important players on the Quibblitch team.

They made me a Creeper. Run told me about Creeper monsters, so at first I thought that I had to go around hissing and blowing people up.

But Markus told me what a Quibblitch Creeper really does. He said that while all the other players are trying to score a goal, I need to creep around looking for a small flying bug called a silverfish. No matter how many goals are scored, if I catch the silverfish, we win the game.

Steve Potter and the Endermen's Stone

Now silverfish are usually just nasty bugs that crawl around on the ground. But they put a spell on this silverfish so it can fly. And when it's flying, it's really hard to catch.

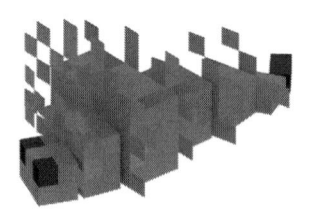

The problem is that silverfish like to bite too. So you need to wear special gloves to handle it, and you have to keep it away from your face. They said that years ago, a really famous Creeper named Tom Brittle was bitten by a silverfish in the middle of a game. It bit his nose right off!

Man, I would hate to be that guy.

As for me, I think I'm just going to fly around and stay away from the silverfish.

Steve Potter and the Endermen's Stone

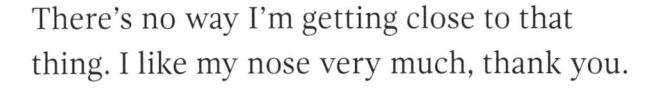

There's no way I'm getting close to that thing. I like my nose very much, thank you.

So, when the game started, I stayed on the outfield just flying on my pig and minding my own business.

All of a sudden Drago flew up behind me and knocked me into the wall. I was so mad that I chased him around the outside of the field.

I knocked him into the wall, and he knocked me back. We just kept flying around the field, knocking each other back and forth into the wall.

Then for some strange reason my pig went crazy! It started to fly around in circles. It shot straight up into the air, and then straight back down. I thought I was going to die.

I waved to Herobriney and Run for help. They started looking around with their binoculars to see if someone was putting a spell on me. Herobriney pointed over to the Spideryn clubhouse, and I saw Professor Snoop moving his mouth. I kept waving my hands for help. What else could I do? Herobriney nodded at me and waved her wand in Professor Snoop's direction.

A few seconds later I saw Professor Snoop catch on fire. *Way to go, Herobriney!* I thought.

My pig stopped spinning and going crazy, but I could tell he was dizzy and not feeling well. I started to guide him down for a landing, but suddenly the silverfish flew in front of my face!

I thought it was going to bite my nose off for sure. So I started swatting my hands wildly to get that thing away from me. It kept chasing me, so I jumped on my pig and flew away as fast as I could.

Steve Potter and the Endermen's Stone

But the silverfish was faster than I was, and it kept swirling around my face trying to bite me. Right when I was going to squash it, Drago came out of nowhere and bumped me really hard into the wall again.

Me and my flying pig came down for a crash landing.

Boy, did I feel dizzy. I felt like I had rocks in my head. And I could hear a ringing in my ears that I couldn't get rid of.

Professor Pooch stopped the game to see if I was OK.

"Are you OK, Steve?" she asked me.

"I'm OK, but I have a lot of ringing in this ear," I told her, pointing to my right ear.

"Let me see," she said. All of a sudden I saw her eyes get really big, and she yelled, "Somebody bring me some tweezers!"

Then she dug the tweezers in my ear as if she were trying to mine for diamonds. She pulled on the tweezers really hard and then, "POP," out came the silverfish!

"Eeewwww!" was all I heard everybody say.

Then Professor Pooch quickly blew the whistle and yelled, "Griffendork wins!"

All of the kids started cheering and patting me on the back. My teammates lifted me up and carried me to the Griffendork house to celebrate. On the way I saw Drago, and I silently mouthed at him, "THANK YOU."

He just gave me a really mean look and walked away.

Chapter 15

A few months later, Christmas Eve arrived. The whole school was decorated like a giant Christmas tree.

"I bet if Santa were real, he would live in a house like this," I told Run, not knowing if he still believed in Santa Claus.

"He does live in a house like this," Run said. "Santa is actually the Professor of Woodworking and Metal shop here at Hogcrafts. We're supposed to take his class next semester. He lives on school grounds."

Whoa. I knew Santa was real, I thought.

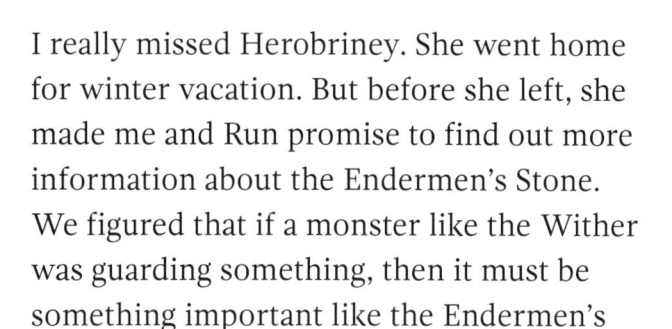

I really missed Herobriney. She went home for winter vacation. But before she left, she made me and Run promise to find out more information about the Endermen's Stone. We figured that if a monster like the Wither was guarding something, then it must be something important like the Endermen's stone, which Haggish was guarding for Professor Bumbledorf.

She told us that we could probably find out more about it in the restricted area in the library.

"How are we supposed to get it from the restricted area in the library?" Run asked. "It's, you know...restricted."

"I'm sure you two can put your heads together and come up with a clever idea. How about sneaking into the library in the middle of the night when Mr. Filth and his cat are eating dinner? Then no one is guarding the entrance to the restricted area in the library," she told us with a smile.

"Oh...Yeah," we both said.

Herobrincy is so smart.

The next day, Run and I jumped out of our beds and ran down to the common room at Griffendork house. We both jumped with joy when we saw all of the presents under the Christmas tree.

"Merry Christmas, Steve," Run said.

"Merry Christmas, Run," I said.

Then we started opening presents.

Run opened up a big box that had a brand new, state of the art, crafting table.

"Whoa, look Steve," he said. Then he crafted a quick pickaxe to test out his new table. "This is wicked! What did you get?"

Steve Potter and the Endermen's Stone

I found my name on a big rectangular chest with a big bow on it. When I untied the bow and opened the chest, I couldn't believe what I saw!

"Whoa!" both me and Run said.

I pulled out a diamond chestplate, a diamond helmet, some diamond leggings and diamond boots. I quickly took them out and put them on.

"How do I look?" I asked Run.

"Bloody smell, Steve, you look awesome!" Run said. "What's that?" he said pointing to a potion bottle with a note on it.

I read the note out loud and it said, "Dear Steve, this belonged to your father. Use it wisely in your search for truth."

"I know what that is!" Run said. "That's an invisibility potion! I heard that when you drink that it makes you invisible for thirty minutes."

"Whoa," was all I could say.

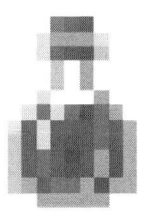

Then me and Run both looked at each other, and I think we were both thinking the same thing.

"Let's drink the potion and go to the girl's dormitory," Run said.

I guess we weren't thinking the same thing.

"No, Run, let's drink the potion and go to the restricted area in the library," I said. "Mr. Filth and his cat won't be able to see us."

"Oh... Yeah. That's a good idea too," he said.

Chapter 16

Later that night, Run and I both drank the potion and we turned totally invisible.

"Remember, Steve, it only lasts for thirty minutes," Run said.

So we walked into the library and looked for the restricted section. When we found it, there was a big gate blocking the entrance.

"Bloody smell, Steve, what are we going to do now?"

I shook the gate to see if I could open it. Then all of a sudden we heard, "Meow!" Following that, we heard Mr. Filth's footsteps close by.

Steve Potter and the Endermen's Stone

"Who's in there?!! Whoever you are, you shouldn't be in this restricted area. When I catch you, you're going to be expelled!" Mr. Filth said.

Run and I tried to sneak out of there, hoping not to get Mr. Filth's attention. We started to creep by him, when all of a sudden, his cat started chasing us.

"Run," I whispered, "the cat can see us."

We started creeping faster until we made it out of the library. But Mr. Filth's cat was still chasing us, with Mr. Filth close behind.

All of a sudden, the potion started to wear off.

"Oh no, the potion is wearing off," Run said.

"Run!" I said.

"What?" Run said.

"Run!" I said.

Steve Potter and the Endermen's Stone

"What is it?" he said.

"No, run!" I said.

"That's my name, don't wear it out," Run said.

A door suddenly appeared in the hallway, so I grabbed Run by his collar and pulled him in behind me.

I cracked the door open and peeked through just in time to see Mr. Filth and his cat run by.

"Whew, that was close," I said.

"How come you didn't just warn me they were behind us," Run said. "We could've outrun them."

I started to see why Herobriney got annoyed with Run all the time.

Steve Potter and the Endermen's Stone

When Run and I turned around, there was a huge mirror standing in front of us.

I walked up to the mirror to get a closer look, and the image changed. I saw two really happy people with a little boy…and he had a scar on his forehead.

"Oh my gosh, Run, I think I see my parents!"

"Whoa. Let me see," Run said.

"Do you see my parents too?" I asked Run.

"No. I see myself!" he said. "And I'm carrying a microphone. And there are millions of people chanting my name! And I'm the owner of Mojang, and I just sold my company to Microsoft for 2.5 billion dollars!"

Steve Potter and the Endermen's Stone

"This mirror must give you whatever you want most in life," I said.

"This is wicked!" Run said.

Then we heard Mr. Filth and his cat coming, so we exited through another door in the back of the room, and made our way back to Griffendork house.

We changed into our pajamas and jumped in our beds.

"What a night, huh, Run? All I can say is that I'm glad it's over. Good night, Run," I said.

"That's Mr. Persson to you," he said.

Chapter 17

After Christmas, the school's halls were filled with the noise of busy students.

One day, when Run and I were studying in the library, Herobriney surprised us with a very thick book.

THUD!

"Here it is, The Book of All things Minecraft, a.k.a The Minecraft Wiki," Herobriney said. "This is where we're going to learn everything we need to know about the Endermen's Stone."

"This book is wicked!" Run said. "Where did you find it?"

Steve Potter and the Endermen's Stone

"In the restricted section, where I told you it would be," she said.

Run and I just looked at each other, embarrassed. Herobriney had a way making us feel like morons because she was so smart.

She thumbed through the pages, and found a section about the Endermen's Stone.

"Here it is," she said, putting a finger on the page, and reading out loud:

The Endermen's stone is a magical stone said to have come from a piece of the egg of an Enderdragon. For centuries the Endermen, guardians of the stone, have kept it hidden from mankind, because of the incredible powers that it possesses.

Steve Potter and the Endermen's Stone

It was said to have been acquired by a gentleman named Nicolas Phlegm, who journeyed into the Enderworld in search of the Enderdragon. Though he did not find the Enderdragon, he managed to trick the Endermen who were guarding the stone into trading the stone to him for a handful of magic beans. Mr. Nicolas Phlegm, through the stone's power, was able to reach the age of two hundred years and amassed a wealth of unknown size.

The Endermen's stone is said to have the power to grant the holder unlimited wealth and unlimited life. It can heal and bring the dead back to life, but it can also destroy life, which makes it both powerful and dangerous. It could even bring forth the end of the world, if it were to fall into the wrong hands.

"I bet you that is what Professor Snoop is after!" I said. "He plans to get the stone in order to bring Lord Baldywarts back from the dead. I saw him with a burn on his arm the day that the mutant Zombie attacked us. He probably let the Zombie in to create a distraction so he could get the stone. But the Wither must've blasted him and burned him."

"That makes sense," Herobriney said. "They say that Lord Baldywarts was once a student here, and he was part of the House of Spideryn. But if Lord Baldywarts actually got his hands on the Endermen's stone, he could destroy the whole world! What are we going to do?"

In my mind I knew what we had to do.

"I hope you are not going to say what I think you're going to say?" Run asked me. "Last time we met up with the Wither, I had to scrub my shorts for weeks to get the stain out."

"We have to, Run," I said. "We need to get the Endermen's Stone before Professor Snoop does."

"But how are we going to get through the Wither?" Run asked.

"Let's look in the book," Herobriney said.

Herobriney turned to the page about the Wither.

"Here it is! The Wither Boss," she said and read it aloud:

The Wither is a floating, three-headed, ghostly mob with a skeletal appearance. The Wither can move very quickly, and upon noticing a person, the Wither attacks with a projectile called the "Wither Skull." Wither Skulls are giant fireballs with the power to destroy any block, except Bedrock and End Portal Frame. It can also destroy Obsidian, which is well known for its immunity to TNT and long mining time.

"That's it!" Herobriney said. "I know what we need to do. We need to push the Wither into a corner and then conjure up a spell in order to surround the Wither Boss with

Bedrock. Then we can go into the trap door unharmed."

"Sounds great, but how are we going to back that monster into a corner?" Run asked.

"I know," I said. "Live bait. Two of us need to distract it, while the other one conjures the spell. Then we need to get out of that corner before we're sealed in with the Wither."

"Let me guess, Herobriney gets to conjure the spell, and you and I have to be the bait," Run said.

"That's the first smart thing you said all day, Run," Herobriney said.

"Oh, man," Run said. "I'd better buy me a new pair of shorts."

Chapter 18

So Run, Herobriney and I went to the West Wing and found the door that led to the Wither.

"You guys sure we should do this?" Run asked. "I mean, the end of the world is not that bad, you know."

"Come on, Run," I said.

So we cracked the door open and instantly heard the popping sound the Wither Boss makes. Except this time it was not as loud.

"Here it goes," I said, and we all rushed in.

"AAAAAHHHH!!!" we yelled as we ran in the door.

Except, instead of the Wither hovering above us, it was locked in a corner, covered in a case of cobblestone.

"Oh, no. Professor Snoop must've beaten us here," Herobriney said.

Then Run got up closer to the stone cocoon covering the Wither. We could still hear it popping in there.

"Wait a minute, I thought the book said that only Bedrock could hold the Wither," Run said.

As soon as Run said that, the Wither blew a piece of the cocoon to bits, and then another part of it to bits. It was getting out!

"We need to get out of here!" I yelled. "Quick, through the trap door!"

Run, Herobriney and I just barely made it through the trap door, when the Wither blew its stone cocoon wide open.

Steve Potter and the Endermen's Stone

"You still in one piece, Run?" I asked him.

"Yup, still dry," he said.

The next thing we had to do was to get through a giant, stone maze.

We started going in different directions, but no matter what direction we went, we hit a wall. After about ten minutes, we got really frustrated.

"What are we going to do?" Run asked. "We've been walking around for a long time, and now we don't know where we're going or how to get back."

"Herobriney, do you have any spells that can show us the way out?" I asked.

"Well, if we were on top of the maze, we could probably have a better view of how to get out," she said. Then she pulled out her wand and said in a loud voice:

"Minecraftium Levitatia!!!"

Then we all start floating up and up until we made it to the top of the maze. From up there we could see the whole maze! And we saw a way to walk around on top of the walls and get out.

It wasn't easy, though, because the walls were really thin. We had to walk very slowly so that we wouldn't fall off.

Steve Potter and the Endermen's Stone

When we finally got to the end of the maze, Run stopped short to keep from falling off of the end of the wall. His sudden stop made Herobriney and I bump into him.

I grabbed onto Run to get my balance, and Herobriney grabbed onto me.

Next thing we know, we all fall off the wall.

"AAAHHHH!!!"

THUMP!

"Is everyone OK?" I asked.

"All in one piece," Run said.

"Not everything," Herobriney said, as she showed us her broken wand.

"Let's just hope we don't have to face any more intensely dangerous challenges," she said nervously.

We all looked at each other and knew we were in trouble.

Chapter 19

After the maze, we came across a long hallway that led to a tall door, and beyond that we found a really high tower. On the walls were blocks that looked like stairs, but they were scattered on different places on the wall. And the only door out was at the very top of the tower.

"I know this!" Run said. "My brothers and I play this at home. This is Parkour! You have to hop on different stones until you make it to the top."

Steve Potter and the Endermen's Stone

Herobriney and I looked at each other in sheer terror because we knew we had to hop all the way to the top.

But then we noticed that there was a lift at the very top, which was probably used to go up and down.

"Look, that must be the lift that Professor Snoop used to get up there," I said. "Run, do you think you can Parkour up there and send it down?"

Run was just happy that he could do something that Herobriney couldn't. So he said smugly, "Of course I can."

So, Run jumped on the first block, then the second, third, fourth and fifth. By the time he hit the tenth block, Run was hopping like a grasshopper on a hot summer day.

He almost made it to the top, but then he stopped.

"What's the matter?" I yelled at him.

"I think Professor Snoop didn't want us to follow him. It looks like someone blasted the last block away," he said. "I'm going to have to jump."

I looked where he had to jump, and it looked like a mile away from where Run was. But Run was athletic, and I think he was a little embarrassed that he would have to give up, especially in front of Herobriney.

So, he went for it.

But... He didn't make it.

Run started tumbling down, and hit his head on one of the stones on the way down. Herobriney gasped, and we just stood there with our mouths open, frozen in terror.

All of a sudden something came over me, and I pulled out my wand and I yelled with all of my might:

"Minecraftium Levitatia!!!"

Run froze in midair, a mere few inches before he hit the ground.

I floated him safely to the ground, and we ran over to him to see if he was OK.

"Oh, no, Steve," Herobriney said, crying. "He's not breathing!"

"Stay with him, Herobriney, I'm going to go get help," I said.

I had been thinking of going back, but I knew it would take too long. So I knew I had to get the Endermen's Stone to see if it could help him.

"I'm going after the Endermen's Stone. I think it might be able to help him," I said.

"Be careful, Steve," Herobriney said.

I pointed my wand up and yelled:

"Minecraftium Levitatia!!!"

Then I floated all the way up to the top of the tower where the door was.

I didn't know what I was getting myself into, or what dangers were waiting for me on the other side of that door. But I had to do something to save my friend.

I just had to.

Chapter 20

When I walked into the room it was dark, but I could see a person in front of the magic mirror that me and Run found the other day. It was the magic mirror that showed you whatever you most desired in life.

But how did Professor Snoop get that huge mirror in here? I thought.

"Professor Snoop, you're not going to get away with this," I said. "I know that you're trying to get the Endermen's Stone to bring Lord Baldywarts back from the dead."

All of a sudden the person snapped their fingers and the door shut behind me. Then all of the torches in the room came on.

Steve Potter and the Endermen's Stone

When I got a better look at him, I realized that it wasn't Professor Snoop. I would recognize that big mound of mussed up, bird's nest hair anywhere.

"Professor Squirrel!" I said.

"That's right, boy. And that is not the only thing you are mistaken about. You see, Lord Baldywarts is not dead!"

He grabbed at the mussed up hair on his square head and pulled it off. Underneath, he was totally bald.

What...?

When he turned around, I saw a weird monster thing attached to Mr. Squirrel's head! It looked like the scariest Zombie parasite that I could ever imagine. It had bulging eyes, nasty teeth, and its nose was missing, like something had bit it off.

Steve Potter and the Endermen's Stone

Then it started talking to me!

"We meet again, Steve Potter, he, he, he," it said.

"Lord Baldywarts!" I said, as I stood there terrified. Then I heard a thunder clap in the distance.

"I see you still have that little reminder of our last meeting on your forehead," he said. Then his eyes started glowing.

Steve Potter and the Endermen's Stone

All of a sudden, my scar started burning.

"AAAHHH!" I fell to the ground in pain.

"You won't get the Endermen's Stone, even if I have to die to stop you," I said. But the pain was so strong I couldn't get up.

"Master, remember, we need him to get the stone," Professor Squirrel said.

Then the pain stopped.

"I will never help you get the Endermen's Stone," I told him.

"Steve, we know that your friend is dying," Professor Squirrel said. "So you need the stone to help heal him. By looking into the magic mirror you can retrieve the stone for us."

I knew he was right. The only way I could help Run was to get him the stone. But I knew that as soon as I got the stone, Lord

Steve Potter and the Endermen's Stone

Baldywarts was going to try to kill me. But I had to try. Run's life depended on it.

"All right, I'll get the stone," I said.

So I walked up to the magic mirror and I looked into it. I saw my parents again, but this time I saw myself at the age that I am now. And I noticed that there was something in my pocket.

All of a sudden, I felt something in my own pocket! I reached my hand into my pocket, and there it was, the Endermen's Stone!

"Now give it to me!" Lord Baldywarts said.

"No, I will not!" I said.

Lord Baldywarts's eyes glowed again, but this time nothing happened.

The stone must be protecting me from Lord Baldywarts's magic! I thought

Steve Potter and the Endermen's Stone

"Your magic won't work on me now that I have the stone," I said.

"Get him!!!" Lord Baldywarts said.

Then Professor Squirrel started to come at me.

I pulled my wand out to float him into the air. But Professor Squirrel snapped his fingers and my wand flicked out of my hand and flew out of the tower window.

Professor Squirrel tried to grab me and get the stone from me. He was too strong for me, so I did the only thing I could think of: I took the stone and touched his forehead with it.

Professor Squirrel screamed.

"AAAHHH!!!" he yelled as he started melting into a puddle right front of me.

He completely disappeared into the puddle, and Baldywarts's spirit shot out of the soup that was left over from Professor Squirrel. Baldywarts flew up in the air.

He floated above me like a giant Wither, and I thought he was going to destroy me for sure.

"I will come back for you, Steve Potter!" he yelled.

Then he flew away, out of the tower window.

Chapter 21

I ran out of the door and jumped on the lift to take me down to Herobriney and Run. I went down so fast, I had to jump out before the lift crashed into the bottom.

When I went over to Herobriney, she was just sitting next to Run crying.

"It's too late, Steve. He's gone," she said.

Oh no, I thought. *Was I too late?*

"Well, let's hope this works," I said as I pulled out the Endermen's stone. I took the Endermen's stone and put it on Run's forehead.

But nothing happened.

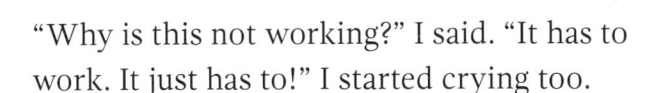

"Why is this not working?" I said. "It has to work. It just has to!" I started crying too.

Then, all of a sudden, "Bloody smell! What happened?!!"

"Run!" Herobriney and I both said, as we jumped on Run and gave him a hug.

"We thought we lost you," Herobriney said, as she and Run looked into each other's eyes. But then they both looked away really fast.

I think the only thing everyone was thinking was, "Awkward!"

But we were all happy that Run was OK.

Then, breaking the moment, we heard a loud popping noise outside.

"Oh, no… You don't think?" I said, because I recognized that noise.

Steve Potter and the Endermen's Stone

We all ran out of the tower and we saw it. At the end of the hallway was the Wither, and it was coming toward us.

"The Wither! It must've found a way out!" I said. "Quick, run back into the tower!"

So we ran back into the tower and shut the door.

Then we heard the Wither shooting fireballs at the other side of the door.

"What are we going to do?" Herobriney asked.

"The lift is broken, and our wands are gone," I said. "I don't know."

BOOM! BOOM! BOOM! SMASH!!!

The Wither finally got through.

It hovered above us, and Herobriney, Run and I just grabbed onto each other.

The Wither made a giant fireball to throw at us.

We just closed our eyes and held onto each other tighter, not knowing what was going to happen.

Then, all of a sudden, a giant flash of light filled the whole room, and then everything went black.

Chapter 22

When I woke up, I felt really groggy.

I looked around, and I could see that I was in the school infirmary. Run was in the bed next to mine, and Herobriney was in the other bed on the other side.

"What happened?" Run asked.

"I don't know. Does anybody remember what happened after the Wither attacked us?" Herobriney asked.

"All I remember was a big flash of light, and then everything went dark," I said.

Steve Potter and the Endermen's Stone

Then, Professor Bumbledorf floated into the room.

"Professor Bumbledorf!" we all said.

"I assume you are all discussing the exciting adventures of the previous evening?" he said.

"Professor, Bumbledorf, Sir, what happened?" I asked. "The Wither was about to throw that fireball at us, and then there was a flash of light, and next thing we know we woke up here."

"It's a lucky thing for you that Professor Snoop is such a snoop," he said. "When he discovered that the Wither had escaped, he came to get me at once. We had just caught up to you, right when the Wither was about to deliver its final death blow to you and your companions."

"Thank you for saving us, Professor Bumbledorf," I said "But what about the Endermen's Stone?"

"We decided to have it destroyed. With Lord Baldywarts alive, there is no telling what he would do to get his hands on it."

Wow, I noticed that there was no thunderclap when he said Lord Baldywarts's name.

"Oh, don't worry. I took care of that too," Professor Bumbledorf said.

Chapter 23

Later that night, Run, Herobriney and I got out of the infirmary, and we ran to the great hall.

"They're going to announce the winner of the Hogcrafts House Cup," Run said. "I hope we win, even though Spideryn has won the Hogcrafts House Cup every year for the past seven years."

"I doubt that we win," Herobriney said. "We were probably docked all of our health points for everything that happened yesterday."

"I'm just glad that we're all OK," I said. Then we all smiled at each other and gave each other hugs.

Steve Potter and the Endermen's Stone

When we got to the great hall, they had just announced that Spideryn had the most points out of all of the Hogcrafts Houses.

The Spideryn kids were all celebrating. As we walked to our seats, Drago gave me a really smug look like he knew he was better than me.

Before they handed the cup to Spideryn house, Professor Bumbledorf stood up to say a few words.

"We want to congratulate Spideryn for another year of being the most exemplary House at the Hogcrafts School of Magic and Witchcraft," he said. "However, this year we have also been blessed with three unique students that have shown admirable qualities in the face of great peril."

"What's he talking about?" Run asked.

"Shhhh!" Herobriney said, as she rolled her eyes.

Steve Potter and the Endermen's Stone

"To Herobriney Stranger, who was willing to sacrifice herself for the sake of her fellow students... I award 10 health points."

"To Run Weasel," Professor Bumbledorf said, and a few students snickered at his name, "for demonstrating determination and strength in the face of danger... I award 10 health points."

"And for Steve Potter, who demonstrated extraordinary courage and bravery, in standing up against an overwhelming evil, all so he could save his dear friends... I give 10 health points."

"And if my calculations are correct, then I am proud to announce this year's Hogcrafts House Cup goes to the house of Griffendork!"

All of the Griffendork kids shouted and cheered.

Run, Herobriney and I gave each other hugs and congratulations.

And Professor Bumbledorf, Professor Snoop, Professor MeGottago and Haggish all gave me an encouraging nod, which made me feel so proud.

...and we all celebrated into the night.

Find Out What Happens Next in...

Steve Potter and the
Cave of Secrets

Coming Soon!

If you really liked this book, please tell a friend right now. I'm sure they will be happy you told them about it.

Please Leave Us a Review

Please support us by leaving a review on Amazon. The more reviews we get the more books we will write!

Check Out Our Other Books from Herobrine Publishing

The Diary of a Minecraft Zombie Book Series

Get The Entire Series on Amazon Today!

The Mobbit:
An Unexpected Minecraft Journey

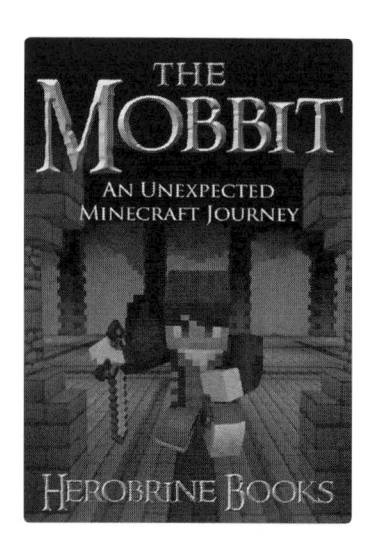

Get Your Copy On Amazon Today!

The Ultimate Minecraft Comic Book Series

Get the Entire Series on Amazon Today!

Ultimate Minecraft Secrets:
Minecraft Tips, Tricks and Hints to Help You Master Minecraft

Get Your Copy on Amazon Today!

The Ultimate Minecrafter's Survival Handbook:
Over 200 Tips, Tricks and Hints to Help You Become a Minecraft Pro

Get Your Copy On Amazon Today!